More Than Just Love

A Devotional For The Foster Care Journey

By Stephanie And Buck Baskin

To all the families who are currently fostering children. We know the journey is hard and thankless at times but we hope you find encouragement and comfort as you continue to do the work God has set you a part to do.

A Special Thanks...

Special thanks to all our friends and family who have loved all our children (foster, adopted and bio), who have rejoiced with us in the good times, and listened as well as lifted us up when things are hard. We could not do this work without you.

Also, a special thank you to DeeAn Thompson who loved our daughter as her first foster mom. She has taught us so much about what it means to be a foster family and to love children from hard places. Her wisdom and friendship is priceless to us.

Front Cover photograph courtesy of Photography by Barnett, Longview, Texas

TABLE OF CONTENTS

FOREWORD

Dear Reader,

I am blessed to have friends like the Baskins in my life and now you get to know them a little bit too! Their heart, perseverance, and commitment encourage me every day. I got a sneak peak into this study and know that they laid their heart bare in hopes that it provides a glimpse into how hard but also how rewarding this work of foster care and adoption can be. I hope that this study encourages you on your journey.

I read an Instagram post the other day. My friend, Sarah, adopted two littles and was sharing the annual "gotcha" day picture. But in it, she chose to confront an issue that I think any of us who work in a service field have heard or felt. Whether you're a social worker, teacher, first responder, foster parent, or pastor, I know you've dealt with this issue. Well-meaning people say something like, "Wow! That's awesome that you do that. I could never." I've heard this my whole career, and frankly for a time I stopped telling people what I do because I didn't know how to respond to this type of reaction. You see, when people say something like that, it feels like they're imposing some sort of superpower on you to hide their own unwillingness to do something. We all know we are no superhero.

We're simply people who said yes when God called. We know that most days we can barely get through the issues we intersect without a deep reliance on His unfailing grace. It is only God who provides patience not to freak out during a storm, who provides the right words during a meltdown, or who simply provides comfort when there is nothing left to do. Those of us who say yes know unequivocally that saying no when God calls is not an option. We say yes because we are intimately familiar with God's grace, the same grace that covers our sins steps in and provides grace in all situations. God's grace is sufficient.

There are some who would encourage you to be a superhero, to take on the issues of the kids that come into your home. If that's what you're looking for, this isn't it. However, if you recognize that you are the best kind of hero, one who said yes to God's call, and need actual Truth to equip you for the work ahead, then you've found the right book. I'm so grateful that instead of saying, "I could never" you chose to answer, "Yes." It doesn't matter if your voice shook or you could only whisper the words out loud. God heard you and He will be with you every step of the way.

The Baskins are people who said yes, too. They've collected some of their lessons learned and shared how God was with them in both tragedy and triumph. This study will encourage you to keep putting one foot in front of the other. Read on and walk confidently into the field of foster care and adoption. God is with you.

Sincerely,

Madeline Reedy
Senior Director, TRAC
www.citysquare.org/trac

Day 1

Believing in the Gospel

"God shows his love for us in that while we were still sinners, Christ died for us."
Romans 5:8

Being a foster family has been the hardest blessing my family has ever chosen to do, and I bet if we could chat face to face you would tell me the same thing. We could swap stories about the good, the bad, the ugly, and even the uglier that comes with the foster care world. I have cried more, laughed more, gotten angrier than ever before, but the one thing I have learned the most is how much our God loves us. He is a BIG God who loves his children BIG.

God sent His son to live amongst humans, sinners, so that the world might be saved through Him. As a foster mom I feel as though it can be hard at times to see good in the world. You hear stories about the most awful things happening to the most innocent of us all, children. It's hard to not get discouraged and if you are like me it's nice to have some encouragement along the way. I personally like to think back on why we decided to become foster parents. We all know the verses that talk about loving the orphans and protecting those who need protecting. Yes, those are excellent reasons to choose to be a foster parent... however, I think none of that matters if we don't know why we love and serve others.

The Bible is clear that God does not like sin. He does not excuse it, but He does forgive it by sending His Son to take our punishment for our sin. When we confess that we are sinners and we need Jesus, only then does He offer His forgiveness. When I think about how big God's love is for me, that He would send His Son to die for me when I don't deserve it, I cannot help but have an attitude of gratitude. I want to show my God how thankful I am for Him that He gave eternal life. Obeying His commands is crucial to showing my love to Him. This is why we became foster parents, not for fame, money or a pat on the back, but to show God how much we love Him by serving and obeying the scriptures.

Today take some time to write down why you became a foster parent/family. Remind yourself of the reasons God has called you to this ministry.

Every child deserves love,
support, & a safe place.

I want to be a mom.

Daily challenge: Though it may be hard, believe
me I know some children with very hard cases,
today look at each child in your home as
someone who needs Jesus. After all, don't we
all need Him and haven't we all sinned? Pray
for opportunities to share His love with those
God brings into your path as you love and
parent a child who is not biologically yours.

Day 2

Redemption For All

For God so loved the world that He gave his only Son. That whosoever believes in Him should not perish but have eternal life.
John 3:16

I am sure that is the first time you have ever heard that verse. While I am clearly kidding in that statement I do want to ask you a serious question.

Have you ever thought about what that verse means? Do you truly believe it?

This verse is saying that Jesus died so that all people who believed in Him could be forgiven, saved. That means ALL people, regardless of where they are from or what they have done. That means that if we are followers of Christ we must believe this to be true. If we believe even one person has done something too terrible to be forgiven and be saved, then according to Scripture that would exclude all of us as well.

What does this have to do with Foster Care And Adoption? As you begin or continue in this journey, you have to realize that you are going to hear some terrible, awful stories. You may hear things that someone would not even put in a movie or crime drama. Those things will break your heart. Those things will make you angry. But guess what? Jesus still died for the people who did those things to the children in your home. Jesus still is offering Salvation and Redemption for the people who said those things to the children in your home. Jesus still wants to restore those people who have harmed these kids and restore the families that are currently torn apart. Let that sit with you for a moment.

I do not know why you got into Foster Care and/or Adoption, or what scares you about it, or what keeps you going. But, I do know that if you are going to do it the right way you, must prepare yourself to live in an attitude that all people and families can be redeemed. Jesus wants to do just that. It's not always going happen, but that is His heart and must be ours as well.

Take a few moments to write down things you think you might hear that someone has done or said, (or things you have already heard from a child in your home) that might cause you to think they have gone too far and can no longer be redeemed. As you write, ask God to change your heart and mind about these things.

_____

_____

_____

_____

_____

Daily Challenge: Take a first step in living with an attitude that all people can be redeemed. Think about a specific instance where you or someone in your life was wronged and you wrote off the person who did the wrong. Today, or in the coming days, release that anger and begin to pray for their redemption.

Day 3

Forgiveness For All

For if you forgive other people when they sin against you, your heavenly Father will also forgive you. But if you do not forgive others their sins, your Father will not forgive your sins.
Matthew 6:14-15

Now that you have mastered accepting that all people and families can be redeemed....

Again, I am kidding of course. This attitude will always be a work in progress, and just when you think you have it all figured out, I am sure another scenario will arise to challenge you, much like with today's study.

You see, just like we have to believe that Jesus wants to forgive all people so that they can be redeemed, we must realize that we too must forgive all people.

This may have been the biggest challenge I faced in the Foster Care And Adoption journey. Mainly because this was something I was not yet prepared to face.

Along our foster care journey I found that the kids in our home, even if they were challenging, became *our* kids. Maybe this is just how our hearts worked, maybe it was because we work with younger kids primarily, or maybe that is just how it is. But regardless, I carried the attitude that the kids in my home were mine for that time period and I wanted them to receive all the protection, love, training, and whatever else that I would give to an adopted or biological child. So one morning when a little girl in our home decided to blurt out some of the things that happened to her in her home you can imagine that the papa bear inside of me wanted to come out.

I will never forget it. It was a Saturday morning and she was finishing her cereal at the coffee table while her older brother and I played Connect 4. Then out of nowhere she begins to share unspeakable things. And what made it even harder was there was no sad music like on TV, no tears, not even any anger. It was like in her mind she did not realize anything she was saying was wrong because it must happen to all kids. I was enraged. No one does things like that to a kid and especially not "my little girl." Of course you cannot freak out in that moment or sound off about the perpetrator in the presence of the victim. But once the dust had settled and we had gathered as much info as we could and made the appropriate calls, I did what I do: I went for a run.

I often will get out and run to clear my head, calm down, or have a quiet time of prayer. But I don't know that any of those things happened on this run. I mean I prayed, but it was not quiet or calming. I prayed out loud, emphasis on the loud. And my prayer was something to the effect of, "God, how could you let this happen!!! Please let me bring justice for this little girl and give me the chance to grab this person who has done this by neck, lift them up, and slam them into a wall!!!" Good prayer, right? You might even cheer that prayer as I am sure others would have as well.

But as often happens in prayer, it is not about us getting what we want or changing God's mind to our will. Instead it is an opportunity for God to change our hearts and minds, and that is exactly what happened here. As I prayed, God began to call the scripture that you just read to my mind. I tried to block it out and yell more, but every time I did, God called it to my mind again as clear as day. To make matters worse, He began to highlight how there were not any qualifications, exemptions, or limitations to this verse. Instead, no matter what happens, I am called to forgive others because I too have sinned. And if I do not forgive others God will not forgive me.

"But God, she is a little kid…" "I know, Buck. It's okay to hurt and be angry and I am far more
13

broken and angered over this than you are. I will take care of it as I have promised you. Your job is to love that little girl and forgive."

And what does it mean to forgive? It does not mean that we accept the sin but instead we show empathy and humility in spirit. We too are sinners in need of forgiveness. There is a chance this perpetrator too was a victim at some point. And through this attitude of brokenness we are able to let go of anger, rage, bitterness, and malice and see clearly God's plan and path for healing. Because this attitude is not just the only way we can truly be obedient to God but also through helping all parties involved find healing and restoration is the only way we are truly going to make kids as safe as possible.

I hope no kid goes through what that little girl went through, but unfortunately one probably will. I also hope you never have to hear stories like the ones I heard from her, but you probably will if you do this for any period of time. Which means you are going to be faced with some hard situations where you have to decide: do you truly believe scripture and are you going to live it out or not? If you wait until the moment comes to make that decision, it will be too late, and not only will you be negatively affected but so will the children in your home.

So I want you to be honest and journal the things that you might see as "unforgivable". They might be things you imagine you might face or could be things you have actually had to deal with in your life. As you journal, ask God to help you be prepared to forgive all people in all situations.

Daily Challenge: Take one situation in your life you have been hanging onto and begin to work towards the process of forgiveness. If appropriate, set a goal of actually talking to that person and forgiving them face to face. If you do not deal with your own difficult situations, you will not be able to properly deal with the ones that children bring with them into your home.

Day 4

A Broken System

Open your mouth for the mute, for the rights of all the unfortunate. Open your mouth, judge righteously, and defend the rights of the afflicted and needy.
Proverbs 31:8-9

Some trust in chariots and some in horses, but we trust in the name of the LORD our God.
Psalms 20:7

Let's just say it, our world, and especially much of the CPS system is broken. On any given day you might deal with, or be affected by, uninformed or unprofessional workers who lack compassion, lawmakers who haven't ever talked to a foster parent or child, lawyers who just want to make money and don't see what is truly best for the child, children who get overlooked, and from time to time even another foster parent might cause more harm than good for the child. So, how do we navigate a system (which to be honest I am glad exists) when you often feel like you are fighting an uphill, never ending battle?

It's like it was just yesterday. It was like a hurricane, tornado, and blizzard hit our home all at once. We had a 6 year old boy living with us. At this particular time, I had to drive him an hour one way to a special school. I would load up the two other little ones and we would make this trip 4 times a day (there and back twice). This particular morning all the storms in him roared at once. I was trying to figure out how to protect all the children in our house and protect him from himself. To make a long story extremely short, he ended up in a psychiatric hospital and would not be allowed back in our home. Our day finally ended at 2 am the next day and all I could think was everyone failed him! I was so mad! We had been constantly telling his CPS caseworker, his counselor, and his lawyer that this kid is about to break. No one who had power seemed to listen.

Another time we had a sibling group whose grandmother was willing to take them, but was denied because she lived in a mobile home. The lawyer on the case did not like mobile homes. She didn't care that grandma loved those kids, could provide for them and had all the resources needed.

Our now adopted son was actually lost in the system. For 5 months we never saw a CPS worker. Our foster agency checked in but no one else did. His case was literally lost. When I would call no one could locate his file.

So back to my original question. How do you navigate a system when you feel as though you are fighting an uphill, never ending battle? When I think about these verses in Proverbs I am reminded of what God wants from us. It will be hard. It will be super frustrating at times. But, if we don't stand in those gaps for our children, who will? We must defend the rights of our children to be loved and taken care of and to live up to their potential.

We must completely put our trust in God. Our trust is not in the CPS system, the judges, the lawyers or even in our own ability. It lies firmly in God. We have been blessed with just as many excellent professionals as we have not-so-excellent ones, but with each child we must put our trust solely in God's hands. There are a few of our kids I still wonder about and pray often that God is protecting them. I know that my worrying heart is peaceful when I truly trust God with each child.

Today I just want to say "keep it up!" I know it's hard. I know that defending your children is not ever easy, but keep doing it. Place your trust in God to give you the strength to go to battle for them. Take a few moments to write down the ways you feel the system is broken.

_____

_____

_____

_____

_____

Daily Challenge: Now take some time to pray and give God full control and trust over each child's case. Pray that He will sustain you and help you keep defending.

Day 5

Seeing God As Good

Give thanks to the LORD, for He is good; His love endures forever.
Psalm 107:1

The journey of Foster Care and/or Adoption can be a messy one. You are dealing with a lot of broken families, broken lives, and broken systems. If you are not careful, all of this brokenness and darkness will drag you down and cause you to lose sight of the one thing that will keep you going. We serve a good God who loves us. Why is this important to remember?

Jesus clearly taught that we are to be a light to the world. Wherever there is darkness you are to come and bring light, hope, and restoration. That is the essence of what every day is in Foster Care And Adoption. But sometimes we get so caught up in all the darkness and brokenness that we merely focus on being broken with the child, being angry at the sin that is destroying their lives, and shouting out about the injustices we are seeing in the world. That is only half the story though, and therefore does no one any good.

We must instead also remember that God is good all the time. God is loving all the time. God's heart is to use us to bring others the hope and restoration that He wants to offer the broken people and systems of the world. So with every moment and every situation we must think, "God, in the midst of this darkness, how do you want to show Your goodness and love, and how is Your goodness and love already here?"

Take the little girl I mentioned a couple of days ago. Clearly there was a lot of brokenness in that story, and it would be very easy to focus on that solely. But if I did, she never gets healing, and I end up getting defeated and quitting. In the midst of being broken for her, I could realize that God never left her. And while her reality is distorted about proper behavior in relationships, in a way, that protected her so she can continue to enjoy the other parts of her childhood while she deals with the effects of these terrible experiences. I can be motivated towards one goal: that God wants me to show her love and bring healing to her no matter how much time she is in my home. I can realize that, as strange as it seems, what is best for her is for her family to be restored and so I can work with the team that is in place and encourage/challenge her parents when appropriate. I can pray like I have never prayed before. I can advocate when no one seems to be listening. All this because I kept my eyes on the fact that no matter what, God is still a good God, a loving God, and I need to make sure that all people from all situations know that.

It does not make things easier, but it does make the work more fruitful and keeps you going for the long haul.

Please know this way of thinking has to be a spiritual discipline that has to be developed. Then as you develop it over time it becomes a natural part of your life so that when those difficult times come you are ready. You need to learn to see how God is good and God is love. You need to learn to take every situation in life, regardless of how messy, and see how God wants to work to make it right to His glory.

To start developing this discipline I want you to take a few moments to journal how you see God's goodness and God's love in the world. You might even want to mix in a few bad things you see in the world and how you believe God wants to work in them.

_____

_____

_____

_____

_____

Daily Challenge: To continue developing this discipline, set a goal that every thirty minutes you will take a moment to pray a prayer of thankfulness for how God is good and God is loving, or to pray that God would show His love and goodness through a specific broken situation.

Day 6

When Others Don't Get It

Jesus went through all the towns and villages, teaching in their synagogues, proclaiming the good news of the kingdom and healing every disease and sickness. When he saw the crowds, he had compassion on them, because they were harassed and helpless, like sheep without a shepherd. Then he said to his disciples, "The harvest is plentiful but the workers are few. Ask the Lord of the harvest, therefore, to send out workers into his harvest field."
Matthew 9:35-38

I can remember when we began our foster care journey. We were super excited and assumed our family and friends would all be as excited as we were. I was surprised at the questions we were asked and how many had to wrap their brain around this idea of foster care. Now, we laugh at some of the questions we have been asked but this was not always the case. The questions used to hurt me. They made me feel lonely wonder if we made the right decision for our family. I am not sure exactly what I expected. I know I wanted everyone to be as excited as I was but that just wasn't the case. (As a side note, we did have supportive family who have walked the road with us as well.)

Maybe it was your friends that weren't supportive. I also learned that not all of my friends would understand; they would ask questions and make comments that were hurtful. If you have dealt with this, I am sorry. I know how hard it is and how when you need people in your corner the most, you can feel abandoned, lost, and hurt.

This makes me think of the verses where Jesus says the harvest is plentiful but the workers are few. Foster care is same. I often feel others don't "get it" because it's so much to take on. It's work that is never done, and can be so overwhelming. Foster parents are the few. I don't say this to brag or be boastful but to acknowledge that the world and sometimes even our churches don't understand.

I have learned over the years that every person I meet who doesn't understand why we do what we do, why we invite chaos into our lives, and why we love children who are not biologically ours (the list continues) we have an opportunity to share God's love. It is an opportunity to share His redemption and His call for us to love the hurting world. I wish I could tell you that every time I was questioned about foster care I took the opportunity to share God's love, but I didn't. What I can tell you is that when I do take the time to compassionately share, God honors it. I also know that not all will understand, and that's ok. Those who don't understand are not personally attacking me, they are struggling with what God's truth says about loving, serving and taking care of others. I now welcome opportunities to answer questions. It's an opportunity to share.

And to those of you who are continually questioned by your family and inner circle of friends, the hard truth is you will have to set up boundaries so the kids in your home will not feel their opposition. But know God hears your prayers and much good will come from you honoring His call in your life. Even Jesus's closest friends questioned Him at times. if Jesus gets questioned we can only assume it will happen to us. Keep doing the work you are doing and keep praying for those in your life who may question you. I pray that through your love and service they will see Christ's love.

_____

_____

_____

_____

_____

Daily Challenge: Pray and ask God how He would want you to answer those who question your decision to foster/adopt. Write it down

and practice it so it becomes second nature.
Pray also that God will allow you to show others
His ultimate love through you. May your words
be seasoned with kindness and truth.

Day 7

Guest Contributor

Brent Mills, Assistant Principal Hallsville Junior High

Roni Mills, Math Teacher Hallsville High School

Brent and Roni are currently foster parents through Buckner CFS East Texas. They have four children Wesley 13, Samuel 12, Daniel 11, and Meadow 3.

Each of you should use whatever gift you have received to serve others, as faithful stewards of God's grace in its various forms.

1 Peter 4:10

This was the verse that God used to get my attention after my family and I had been praying about becoming a foster family. The Lord convicted my wife that we needed to be more active in our faith and we needed to help His children, then he worked the in hearts of our 3 biological children. I on the other hand was very stubborn and thought that God was using us just the way we were. My wife and I are both educators and have seen our share of tragic situations in the home lives of some of our students, and after much prayer I came across this verse while studying for a Sunday school lesson and those situations kept coming to my mind; I was all in and the journey started.

Being a foster family is the hardest but most fulfilling thing I have ever done in my life. We have been fostering for over 3 years and have had over 11 placements, one of which led to the adoption of our first baby girl, Meadow. She is such a joy; if I hadn't listened to the Lord I would have been robbed of one of my greatest blessings.

We have also fostered 3 children that were in kindergarten when they came into our home and started in the same district in which we teach; this has been one of the most challenging aspects of our journey. For example, our biological boys have been in zero trouble during their early school days and have never been in the principal's office; within the first 3 days for getting our first kindergarten boy he was in the office 3 times, suspended and then put into ISS (in school suspension). This trend happened in all 3 of our school age kids and each time I doubted if I could handle these types of situations. In every weak moment I get into the Word and I am reminded that God is near and I should never grow weary of doing His work.

Defend the weak and the fatherless; uphold the cause of the poor and the oppressed.

Psalm 82:3

Brent and Roni Mills

Day 8

Finding Your Support

Rejoice with those who rejoice, and weep with those who weep.
Romans 12:15

My wife has a saying, "Nobody cries alone." This honestly came out of the fact that it seemed like wherever we were, whether working at a bookstore together or volunteering at the church, if someone needed to cry they seemed to find her and she ended up crying with them. But as we have gone through the Foster Care And Adoption journey, we have had to expand that saying to, "Nobody does life alone."

While this is true for everyone, it is especially true for people like you who are on the Foster Care and/or Adoption journey. You cannot do this alone. You are going to need people to rejoice with you, people to cry with you, You are going to need people with whom to vent, people to help fill in your gaps in knowledge, and people to encourage you. Simply put you are going to need lots and lots of people, and I am not just talking about the army of lawyers, caseworkers, and counselors that will be a part of your journey with almost every child.

I wish I could say we fully understood this going in. My wife is a Licensed Master's Social Worker who has worked with foster kids in every job and internship she has held. I am a school teacher. We both had worked in churches, and we both have volunteered for years in the student ministry. So, we kind of felt like between the two of us that we had this all figured out. But thankfully, through a few circumstances along the way, we began to learn the lesson that we need an ever expanding support system. I will give you just a few examples that hopefully will help you begin to think about who might need to be in your support system and the kinds of people you might need to begin reaching out to in order to continue to grow your support system.

One night in our training classes we talked about having a survival kit so that any moment you would be ready for a kid to come and at least get them through the night. Everyone started discussing with each other the things they could get out of the attic or rearrange. There was one problem though. We did not have any kids and therefore had nothing to get out of the attic. Thankfully though we were able to reach out and friends gave us clothes, toys, bottles, and so much more.

Our first placement was a 3 year old boy and a two week old baby. I got the call from my wife at work that this was going to happen. While I was excited I also started freaking out. Why? I had never even changed a diaper. But thankfully a friend of mine was there who immediately asked when the kids were coming, which was later in the evening. He proceeded to tell me to call my wife and meet him at Babies 'R Us after work. He walked us through what to buy, what to give them when, and what we did not need. He was even readily available for a phone call when we had big questions. Questions like "Should we call the doctor?", "Do you have to use special dish soap to wash bottles?" (You have to use special laundry detergent for babies, why wouldn't you use special dish soap?)

Sometimes it is smaller things. Those two children were Hispanic. Thankfully God had blessed us and continues to bless us with a diverse life group. Out of that group, there were people who simply spoke Spanish to the kids. You could see how it gave a little extra special brightness to their day. Another friend made the little boy Spanish rice. You would have thought that we had never fed him before the way he vacuumed it up.

At one point we thought we were going to adopt those two children but to make a long story short, it fell through in the worst way. Basically, in the morning we thought we were heading

33

down the road to adoption and then 6 hours later the children were going home. In the long run this was all for the best, but needless to say in the moment we were devastated. A couple of days later our agency was discussing the story in a staff meeting. As one of the adoption counselors heard that story and decided to call us. She came over to our home, sat there for two hours, let us tell the story, and listened to our anger and heartache. While we did not fully get over the pain that night, I know that without those two hours we might never have healed and moved on.

A few days after that of the girls in my wife's small group got all the girls from the group together. They came over and surprised my wife by taking her out to lunch, taking her to get her nails done, and just to remind her that they were thinking about her and that she was loved.

I could go on and on about stories of family members, people at church, and random strangers who have been a part of supporting us and the kids in our lives throughout this journey. Hopefully you can begin to see how vital it is to have a support system.

You may have already seen today's journal assignment coming, but I want you to begin to write down the people in your support system and those who could be in your support system. If you see gaps, brainstorm how you might close those gaps.

_____

_____

_____

_____

_____

Daily Challenge: If you are just beginning the Foster Care and/or Adoption journey, begin the process of reaching out to your support system and building that network. This could be friends, professionals, co-workers, family members, or anyone else God brings across your path. Explain to them what you are doing, why you are doing it, and why you need them. If you are already in the journey and don't have a support system, build one immediately. If you have one, take the time to thank them for what they mean to you in this journey via text, email, phone call, letter, or face to face.

Day 9

Understanding Their Reality

*Do not love this world nor the things it offers
you, for when you love the world, you do not
have the love of the Father in you. For the world
offers only a craving for physical pleasure, a
craving for everything we see, and pride in our
achievements and possessions. These are not
from the Father, but are from this world. And
this world is fading away, along with everything
that people crave. But anyone who does what
pleases God will live forever.*
1 John 2:15-17

"Oh, that's just what daddies do." I have a
Master's in Social Work, my license in social
work, I worked for several years with teens in
foster care who were aging out, did group
counseling, and the list goes on. However,
none of this prepared me for the night I was
bathing a three year old girl. She and her
brother had been with us for about 2 months.
They both had larger than life personalities and
we were still adjusting to each other. On this
night, she began to talk and share details of her
story I had not heard. As she talked, I began to
cry. She noticed my tears and asked, "Why are
you crying?" When I told her it was because it
made me sad to hear how these things had

happened to her, and that no little girl should have those things happen she said, "Oh that's just what daddies do."

The magnitude of her words did not hit me until later. How could she not know daddies should never do such things to their little girls? They are supposed to love them, protect them, have tea parties and take them to the movies or ballgames. Not this! The more I thought about this, the more I realized her reality is so different from mine. She sees the world so differently. Her line of good and bad is skewed because those previously caring for her were not offering her a love from God, but a love full of evil, which is not a love at all.

I would like to tell you I remembered this every time she acted out or had a larger than life melt down, but I didn't. I did however find a new attitude towards her behavior as a whole. I had to take time to see the world as she had seen it for her first 3 years of life. A life where, as the scripture above states, those who "cared" for her had only "a craving for physical pleasure, a craving for everything [they saw]".

Today take some time to write down some ways your kids have a different reality than you.

_____

_____

_____

_____

_____

Daily challenge: Pray God will show you how to show His love to your kids even when it seems impossible, and how you can help them have a new reality.

Day 10

More than Love

When Moses' hands grew tired, they took a stone and put it under him and he sat on it. Aaron and Hur held his hands up—one on one side, one on the other—so that his hands remained steady till sunset. So Joshua overcame the Amalekite army with the sword.
Exodus 17:11-12

Sometimes there are kids who make a lasting impression on you. Even when they leave your home, you do things differently because you learned so much from their time with you. When we first started our classes to become foster parents we learned all about the difficult situations that little ones will have endured. We read case study after case study of abuse. I kept telling myself God has prepared me and my husband for this journey. I had all the book knowledge in the world. I had the degrees, and, together, we could love kids from hard places and help guide them to healing.

One of my biggest issues with working in the system was seeing so many kids on medicine. Many taking cocktails of medicine. It became my mission to make sure we did our utmost due diligence and did not use medicine. I think I believed we could show them love, show them how to handle their emotions and could give them tools to make medicine unnecessary. I remember sitting in doctors appointments and ARD meetings advocating and pleading for my child not to be placed on medicine. I thought I was protecting him. I thought it was in his best interest. He was so little, only 6.

This little one did end up on medicine after a series of events. I felt like I had lost. I felt like it was a personal failure. Within His first week on the anxiety medication, we began to see a new kid. A child who was laughing, and using his tools learned in counseling to calm down. A child who was polite and an absolute joy in our home.

I finally understood why kids in care need a team working together to help them succeed. I could show him love all day long but he needed more than what I alone could give him.

This reminds me of a story in the Old Testament. God told Moses all he had to do was hold up the staff while Joshua and his army fought the Amalekites. As long as the staff was in the air the army would continue to win. When Moses got tired, Aaron and Hur gave him a stone to sit on and held his hands up for him. As a result the Israelites won the battle.

Moses needed a team to help him succeed. Our kids do too. We, as foster parents, can get tired and may not always know the best answer. I have heard, "I just have so much love to give to help kids." I know I've even said it myself. While this is true, we must remember true love looks like Aaron and Hur holding up Moses's arms for him when he was weary. These kids are in a huge battle. We as foster parents will feel like Moses at times. Use your team: Medicine, CPS, your agency, counselors, friends family,etc. These children deserve a full army fighting for their future!

Take some time today to write out the challenges the child(ren) in your home are dealing with at this time.

_____

_____

_____

_____

_____

Daily Challenge: Pray and ask God if there are professionals or others you need on your team. Ask them to join you in your kids battle. If you already have a team, thank God for them and for the part they are playing in fighting the battles for your child(ren).

Day 11

Humility

Pride goes before destruction,
a haughty spirit before a fall.
Proverbs 16:18

I mentioned a few days earlier that there was a
time early on in this journey where my wife and
I felt that based on our knowledge and
experience we had this all figured out. That
attitude has a name, Pride. And as today's
scripture says, pride will lead you to destruction
and failure. The journey of Foster Care and/or
Adoption really highlights this truth. If you are
going to be successful in this journey and stay
in it for the long haul, you must remain humble.
Your need for God and a team of other people
will be evident. There will always be areas of
growth and change.

The greatest example of this for me is caring for
a five year old boy with 16 year old emotions. I
can honestly say he was not a bad kid at all. He
simply saw that his family was not together and
took the blame and weight of that loss on his
own shoulders. That is a heavy burden for
anyone, let alone a five year old. This
manifested in massive outbursts and tantrums.
We had never seen anything like it. At first, it

started as hour long tantrums because he wanted to play instead of do homework. Then they stretched out to two hours. We did not think too much of it at first. Pride told us that we had worked with teens, we had been through training for foster care and for our professions, and we knew every behavior modification strategy in the book. But, there is something different about all of it when the kid is in your home. When you start to say you have it all figured out get ready to learn a lesson.

For us, this lesson began to come as the fits got bigger and longer. One of the last ones I can remember was a battle from 10:00 a.m. until about 9:00 p.m. He finally relented and decided he would go to bed. There were little breaks in between, but for the most part it was a constant battle. Part of the reason it got this bad was because we kept trying to figure it out on our own, because we knew it all. To compound that we had also set some do not cross boundaries in our minds. One of those was no medication. Our intention was pure. We had seen too many kids put on meds who did not need them. We had also seen the effects medication had on them. But the other part of it was we "knew" we could figure out a way to help a kid change without medication because we were "experts." Needless to say, the day came when we finally had to take him to a psychiatric care hospital.

The fits would not stop, and he was putting himself in danger. I cannot tell you how defeating that felt. It was so hard to leave a five year old in that situation. But God used this situation for God. For one, the child received some help and strategies that he desperately needed. Also, he was connected with the right doctors and ended up getting on the right medication. While I still am hesitant to put any child on medication, I know now sometimes they really need it. Medication did not stop him from getting mad, but it did cap him off at a certain point so we could still talk to him and he could implement the strategies he was learning to calm himself. Basically it gave him a chance to be successful. We also were offered more training to help us understand trauma and its effects on children, training that I am sure we would have been offered much sooner if we had only admitted we needed help[1].

Quick disclaimer: I do not want you to hear that if you are humble it will be all smooth sailing. There is a good chance because of what this kid was dealing with he may have ended up needing counseling and treatment no matter what we did. I can guarantee that at some point you will face situations that seem more difficult

---

[1] I know trauma is kind of a buzzword now but at this time it was not. So while many of you may get sick of hearing about it, I encourage you to get all the training on trauma and its effects that you can. Because it affects all of us, and especially kids from hard places.

than you can handle. You may feel defeated. But what I can promise you is that if you will continue to humble yourself daily, reach out to God and others for strength, and be willing to do whatever is necessary for the children in your home, they will find healing. Not only that but you will also be successful in showing these children that they are loved, and you will be able to stay committed to this journey for the long haul.

Today, take a few moments to think through areas where you tend to struggle with being prideful.

_____

_____

_____

_____

_____

Daily challenge: Pray for humility in these areas. Find someone to confess to, ask them to point out areas you missed, and ask for accountability to remain humble.

Day 12

No Control

Many are the plans in a person's heart, but it is the Lord's purpose that prevails.
Proverbs 19:21

Ok, it's time for me to confess. Becoming foster parents seemed like a no brainer for us. I spent 6 years going to school learning about people. I interned with a foster care agency. My job at the time was as a case manager with teens who were going to age out of the system. Y'all, I knew the system front and back! I knew the policy. I heard the cries of the kids in care. I heard the heartache from foster parents. I *had* this! I had this idea that because of my experience and knowledge caseworkers, judges, lawyers, teachers, etc, would value my opinion, listen to what I thought was best, and make decisions based on what I suggested.

Are you laughing yet? I laughed just writing this. The foster care/adoption world leaves little room for control by the foster parents. I can remember crying when I felt unheard, when CPS made a decision without consulting me, or when (let's call it like it is) I had no control. Don't these people know who I am and what I know? It was super upsetting to me.

46

Maybe You have felt like this too. It is as if you have no control over your situation or the decisions being made for the children in your home. I mean, you are the one with them 24/7 why won't "they" listen to you?!

God has taught me many things in our adventures of fostering (and adoption) but none more than to really trust Him. If we truly trust Him then we automatically give up control. He is in control. He created the earth (Genesis 1:1), knows the number of hairs on our head (Matthew 10:30) and He is the only one who knows when He is returning (Mark 13:32). I know He has the ultimate say. I could wrap my brain around trusting God but I would say jokingly "I trust God but I don't trust others." The truth is I didn't completely trust Him. If I did, I would spend less time trying to control the situation and more time praying for His will and wisdom for each child in my home.

Please understand. There are times to advocate for your child. You should absolutely tell your caseworker your thoughts and your opinions about what is best. What I learned, however, is God is a big God. And I had to allow myself to trust each child to Him. When I did this, I found my heart changed. I was less concerned about controlling and less angered when I felt unheard. I spent more time on my knees praying for the future of each child. Through prayer I felt confident that even though others may not be listening and I may feel out of control, God hears my cries and HE HAS THIS!

_____

_____

_____

_____

_____

Daily Challenge: Spend some time writing out the situations you are experiencing with your kids where you feel you have no control. Pray over these areas. Pray God will hear your heart for your kids. Pray He will protect their future and that those making the decisions will listen to you. Pray for less need for control and more trust in Him who created everything.

Day 13

Righteous Anger

Be angry, and yet do not sin; do not let the sun go down on your anger, and do not give the devil an opportunity.
Ephesians 4:26-27

If you have not noticed, I (Buck) have gotten most of the lessons about being mad. That is because before foster care I thought I was a very easy going. That I let it all roll of my shoulders. Then we started dealing with a dark and sinful world. I quickly found out I still had a lot of anger inside of me.

Maybe, you will find out the same thing. Do not be discouraged. As we can see from the Bible today it is clearly okay to get angry. Why else would the Bible say be angry yet do not sin? This is not something we often think about in the church, or in our culture in general, but there are things in life that should make us mad. Sin destroying lives, the injustices of the world, disease, and the list goes on. As you continue on this journey of Foster Care and/or Adoption, you will quickly find many more things to add to your list.

You will hear terrible stories of what has happened in kids' lives. You will also have to deal with the ignorance of others around you (even people in your church and biological family). Parents will not come to visits. School systems may not understand how to deal with the special circumstances some of the children in your home will bring. People in the system may fail to do their job, and it will negatively affect you and the children in your home. Grownups will make decisions that greatly affect a child without even talking to the child... And guess what, in these moments where you see children are being hurt, or their lives are being destroyed, it is okay to get angry! Let that free you for a moment. When you feel angry in situations like these, you do not have to feel guilty. In fact you should feel encouraged because your heart is open and in tune to the things that anger and break God's heart as well.

Take a few moments to list out the things you feel Christians should be angry about. Make sure to include a few examples of foster care specific situations.

_____

_____

_____

_____

_____

Daily challenge: Pray over the injustices in the world you mentioned and cry out to God about them. Let Him know how it angers you and breaks your heart. Tell Him why. Thank Him that He cares about the lost and the broken far more than we do. Cry out for Him to use you to bring healing to a lost and dying world and to move in a mighty way in the world around you.

Day 14

Guest Contributor
Andi Harrison, Director Of Foster Care &
Adoption at Buckner International

Andi not only works at Buckner helping families like ours in their foster care journey but her and her husband are currently foster parents. Andi has been a huge resource to our family as we navigate the foster system.

And he was moved with compassion for them....
Matthew 14:14

I have worked in child welfare for seventeen years in a variety of different positions, but the one thing that remains constant are traumatized children and foster parents. People choose to be a foster parent to love a child and to make a difference. The world thinks you hung the moon. However, on any given day the children you are caring for could be having a meltdown because their biological parent didn't come for a visit, getting a call from the teacher that the child is failing or you learn that the children have been sexually acting out with one another. You feel like a failure. Your compassion meter is on empty. It is easy to run low on compassion with the daily grind as a parent much less a foster parent.

However, I want to encourage you to stay focused on the child's history. The child's history with the help of the Holy Spirit will produce compassion. Scripture is clear that when Jesus showed compassion there was healing. The children are looking for compassion even when they do not know what it looks like. They are looking for the hug that you give them after they hit you. They are looking for the "I love you" after they screamed at you that you aren't their parent. They are looking for the fist bump after their visitation. Those simple things shows compassion. You are teaching the child compassion. You are healing them.

As you are showing and teaching compassion, God is at work in your life! God is healing you as well. God is changing you and changing your family. You are no longer the same family that you were before your first placement. As a social worker, I love to see families change over time. Your love for others looks different. Your compassion for those around you is deeper. Your hope for the future is bright.

I want to take a moment to thank you for being obedient to God. Thank you for allowing the Holy Spirit to produce curiosity to come to the first informational meeting about foster care. Thank you that the Holy Spirit gave you the perseverance to continue when you felt like a failure. And most importantly, thank you for making a difference in a child's life where they were able to see God's love for them through your actions.

Andi Harrison
Director of Foster Care & Adoption at Buckner International

Day 15

Unrighteous Anger

Be angry, and yet do not sin; do not let the sun go down on your anger, and do not give the devil an opportunity.
Ephesians 4:26-27

I am fully aware that I used the same scripture twice. This was done intentionally, because there is so much to unpack in just this one verse.

The other day we focused on being angry. I hope your were encouraged to know that you can get angry about things. But we also need to realize that if we can be angry and not sin, than there must be times where we are angry and do sin.

Some we sin when we are angry about the wrong things. Other times, we respond in the wrong way when we are angry about the right things. There are so many examples I could use to explain how anger could lead to sin. But I want to highlight one specific moment you may unfortunately face far too often as a foster/adoptive parent.

Parents may not show up to visits. There are a lot of tough moments you will face as a foster parent, but this is one of the toughest for me. IU hate how it blindsides the child. You will show up with them at the expected time. They will have been talking all day about seeing their parents because they know it is visit day. You will be watching the child wait excitedly at the chosen location for the visit. Then, without warning, a case worker, or someone, will come in and say mom/dad/grandma, or whomever are not coming. Imagine being a kid in that situation and how disappointed you now feel. You have already been removed from your home and now mom or dad, for whatever reason, are not coming for the one moment you get to see them, play with them, hug them. Regardless of what has happened, think about what that must do to a kid. Now think about what you are going to feel in that moment. You see a kid angry, crying and broken. At some level you are going to get angry, which is okay, because you are seeing how sin is destroying the lives of people in this world. You are angry because you know this is not right. But how do you respond?

First, let's deal with the sin. One of your initial reactions will be to want to bash mom and dad because that is just what we as humans want to do. In your mind, you may also think that by tearing down mom or dad, the kid will realize this is not their fault. But guess what? It doesn't work that way. Because the bigger picture that is taking shape here is that is still their mom and/or dad, and the ideal situation is that someday that child goes home. Ideally the family is reunified and your unkind words would do nothing to help work towards that end goal. You might also want to just say "let's stop doing visits since the parents are not showing up anyways". For one, this is not in your control so it is not really an option. But also take a moment to think about this. By saying that you not only are hurting the child but you also are saying the parent and this family are beyond redemption. Does that sound like a biblical, Christ-like attitude? So what can you do?

First, allow your heart to break with the kid. Listen to them and what they are feeling. You can also be patient. There is a good chance they may act out behaviorally and emotionally the rest of the day. You also could be proactive by having a plan in place in case mom and/or dad do not show. This could be as simple as having a toy in the car they love and do not know is with you. Or an impromptu ice cream trip works wonders! Depending on the kid a movie when you get home, or a trip to the park to burn off steam can be effective as well. If possible try to figure out why the parents are not showing up and see if you can help in some way, including being flexible on the scheduling and location. Also, again if possible, I encourage you to talk to the parents (when the kids are not listening) and in an encouraging and loving way let them know how important these visits are to their child, how much they look forward to them, and how important it is that they do everything in their power to be there. Also let them know you are praying for them.

Basically what this boils down to is, just like any situation in life, we are faced with two paths. One is sin and one is not. The question is, which path will you choose?

Today take a few moments to write down times when you have been angry and sinned. Begin to pray a prayer of confession and ask for the strength to grow and change. Also, write down a few things that are not worth getting angry about as a reminder. A few things to consider might be a kid refusing to eat vegetables, a case worker showing up late, or a new policy getting added to minimum standards.

_____

_____

_____

_____

_____

Daily Challenge: Begin to workout some plans for the difficult moments you may face in foster care and how you can be proactive so that you might be angry and not sin. Family visits is one area, but it could also be bad behavior days, late night placements, bad decisions by caseworkers, etc.

Day 16

Reunification When You Don't Agree

*Know therefore that the LORD your God is God,
the faithful God who keeps His covenant and
steadfast love with those who love Him and
keep His commandments, to a thousand
generations,*
Deuteronomy 7:9

*Do you not know? Have you not heard? The
Lord is the everlasting God, the Creator of the
ends of the earth. He will not grow tired or
weary, and His understanding no one can
fathom.*
Isaiah 40:28

One of the most common questions hear is,
"How do you send them back to the family when
you don't think it's what is best for them?" This
is a valid concern, and it can be one of the
hardest experiences. To pack up a child who
you have loved and cared for and send them
home to someone you are not sure will do the
same us an awful, emotional journey. You
wonder, are they going to be safe? Are they
going to get the care they need? Will they have
food?

I still wonder about kid we sent home over 6
years ago. I still think of these children and

wonder if they are safe, what they would look like and if they had a meal today. The short end of a long story is mom asked us to adopt her kids, we hired a lawyer, we went to court, she changed her mind, we get kicked out of court (still don't know why), and the kids went home 4 hours later. Why? Two weeks ago mom didn't want them. A week ago she was asking if we would adopt them. There were so many reasons we felt it was not in the children's best interest to return home. I cried. I yelled. I yelled at everyone - caseworkers, Buck, the lawyer, and at God. How could God let this happen? How could a system that is supposed to protect children, fail? These were my raw emotions.

I am sure you can think of the children you packed up as well. How do we reconcile this with God? And,like me, you may even ask where is God in all of this?

So I don't have the answer. I have learned, though, we must place our trust in God. If we believe in Him then His word is true. We must cling to His promises especially in these times of doubt. Here are a few of my favorite verses. They bring me peace when I don't understand the why's. I hope they are a comfort to you as well.

Know therefore that the LORD your God is God, the faithful God who keeps His covenant and steadfast love with those who love Him and keep His commandments, to a thousand generations,
Deuteronomy 7:9

Do you not know? Have you not heard? The Lord is the everlasting God, the Creator of the ends of the earth. He will not grow tired or weary, and His understanding no one can fathom.
Isaiah 40:28

It's not always easy and I have cried tears over my little ones too. Today take some time and memorize one of these verses to hide in your heart, to cling to when you don't understand why.

Use this space to to write about some of the situations you didn't understand. Ask God to show you where He was in those times.

_____

_____

_____

_____

_____

Day 17

Dealing With Fear

For God has not given us a spirit of fear, but of power and of love and of a sound mind.
1 Timothy 1:7

When studying scripture we are often reflective. What does this passage mean in the historical context it was written in? How would that apply today? What does this really mean? While those are good strategies, sometimes we need to realize that some passages are just clear promises with no wrestling and reflecting required. This is one of those passages.

We have not been given a spirit of fear. When we feel fear coming, we know that through the power of the Holy Spirit inside of us and through loving God and loving others, we can see clearly and overcome that fear. Period. End of story. Let that fire you up right now. There is nothing to be afraid of. Let that empower you. No matter what challenge you face in life, and particularly in the journey of foster care/adoption, you do not have to be afraid.

Even still, because we are not perfect, there are times when we will be afraid. So I want to share a few moments where I was afraid and the lessons I learned. Hopefully these stories will help you deal with fear better than I did.

One are that we have dealt with fear repeatedly is when kids go home. Often times when they go home it is perfectly clear it is the right decision. Sometimes it is not so clear. Either way it is always an emotional day and for us one of the biggest emotions is fear. Sometimes we have felt fear because the biological parents lived close to the kinship placement and we were not sure the proper boundaries would be in place to protect the child. At other times, like with our first placement, we knew it was great they went home. We had all grown attached to each other due to the length of the placement and other unique factors in this situation, so it was almost like it was our kids going to someone else's home. We could not help but wonder and fear about what was happening. But what did that fear get us? Nothing but stress. And what did that fear boil down to? A lack of trust in God. You see we were not fully trusting that God had a plan, that He would protect those children, and work in their lives. We also did not humble ourselves to realize God loves those children far more than we could and knows far more about what is best for them than we do. This also means that deep down we were not truly living in love because we were wanting what we wanted, instead of what God wanted.

Another time you might face fear is with the kids in your home, regardless of the age of child you are bringing in. For example, at one point we had a six year old in our home. He began to act out in anger at school and at home. Eventually he began to direct his anger towards our soon-to-be-adopted daughter. We felt a lot of fear. How do we keep all our kids safe? What happens if people do not listen to us about how dangerous he is? How do we react if something does happen? Looking back, I realize that this fear boiled down to a lack of trust that God would take care of all the kids in our home Now this does not mean we should not have been aware of the situation and be proactive as we were as putting in safeguards to protect all kids, as well as communicating to caseworkers and other parties that were involved. To me that is part of being loving and of a sound mind. But there was no need for fear and the fear did us no good. I also realize, no one called us out on our fear. We as Christians must hold each other accountable to live out the scriptures that we know to be true and form trusting, deep relationships so we are ready to receive this accountability. This is especially true in cases where our behaviors, like fear, make sense to the world.

The other major time we faced fear may surprise you because it surprised us. It was on national adoption day when we adopted our middle child. National adoption day is one big party filled with balloons, matching family outfits, laid back judges, and lots of celebration. So how in the midst of all of that could we be afraid? We had had an adoption fall through. So we knew nothing was final until the judge banged his or her gavel. We also knew that, because of how the system works sometimes, you never know when an investigation might pop up. So while everyone around us was having fun celebrating all we could think of was get us to the courtroom and bang the gavel. Eventually the gavel banged, and our daughter was ours forever. But leading up to that left fear control the situation instead of having fun. I missed the celebration with my family and others. All because of fear.

Fear will come. This is natural. Again, like anger, I would say do not feel bad when fear comes. Emotions are natural and normal. But how do you respond to them? Do you let it cripple you or make you shy away from opportunities to do what God is calling you to? Or do you see it as a lie from Satan and use it as an opportunity for love, power, to think clearly, and to serve God in a mighty way?

I cannot predict what will cause fear in your experience. To get ahead of the game, take a moment to write down the things about foster care/adoption that cause fear in you. Be honest about what scares you on this journey so that you will be ready to be an exponentially greater foster/adoptive parent.

_____

_____

_____

_____

_____

Daily Challenge: Pray that God will provide peace during these times of fear.

Day 18

Investigations

*"When you are brought before synagogues,
rulers and authorities, do not worry about how
you will defend yourselves or what you will say,
for the Holy Spirit will teach you at that time
what you should say."*
Luke 12:11-12

God knows what is going to happen, He knows
when, and as long as you are serving Him and
aligned with what He is calling you to do, He will
give you what you need when you need it.

To me that is the heart of this verse and why it
is so powerful as a follower of Christ in general,
but especially as a foster/adoptive parent. You
will come under attack spiritually and in a very
earthly sense, which we could argue are
spiritual attacks as well. You just need to accept
that fact. But you also need to accept that God
will be with you in those times. This is especially
true when it comes to investigations.

Investigations happen to almost all foster
parents at one point. Even with though they are
so common, they may be one of the most nerve
wracking things that can happen to you as a
foster parent. Because of this, I want to try and

offer you a little encouragement through scripture and through some practical advice. So I will provide a few words on how to "survive" an investigation, why investigations occur, what happens during an investigation and a few tips on what to do.

For me, there are three keys to dealing with an investigation. The first is you have to realize that at some point they happen to everyone. So when you get a call from licensing that you are under investigation do not feel like a failure or go into a panic. It is just part of the journey. Second, you need to remember that the kid placed in your home is not your kid. They are under the state's jurisdiction and on top of that the parent's rights have not yet been terminated. Even though you are making all the medical decisions, educational decisions, driving to visits and practices, dealing with the fits, and handling the emotional stress of the situation they are in on top of the emotions they are dealing with simply because of their life stage, they are not officially your kid. This realization helped me to release a lot of anger and fear. It is understandable that someone would want to do everything they can to make sure the kid is safe, and I would want the same for my kid. Along with that, even though a parent may be making terrible decisions, deep down that is their kid and they know they want to protect them and make this work, even though there may be other things from their past or present factors that are hindering them from fully doing so. Third, investigations are a good thing because at some point someone did do something wrong when caring for a foster child. So someone saw fit to put in place a process to ensure these kids are being properly looked after and cared for.

The next big question when it comes to investigations is usually, "Why do they occur?" Or, "What could bring an investigation to my house?" It can be for all sorts of reasons. We have had two investigations and they were both because a child chose to run away from our home. Another foster parent we knew came under investigation because she took the foster children out to visit her family for the weekend. While the foster children were playing, one of her biological children's cousins pulled out a BB gun and a foster kid got shot in the leg.[2] We have had other friends come under investigation because there was a pre-existing medical condition when the child came into the home. When the foster parent took the child to the doctor they found something the foster parent was unaware of that could have been related to the pre-existing condition. So they came under investigation to ensure they were not neglecting

---

[2] If you did not grow up in the country please know that this is not as big of a deal as it sounds.

the child. We have also heard investigations may occur because the parent has a complaint or the child makes an accusation of abuse against the foster parent. Now, if you are starting to get scared, please remember that we are not supposed to be afraid. Most of the time these investigations come pass very quickly. You go about your lives and the child at most gets moved to a different home temporarily while the investigation occurs.

As far as what to expect, I can only speak from our limited experience. As mentioned before, on two separate occasions, we had different six year old boys run away. A six year old running away is a scary experience. When it happened to me the boy's sister was in the house as well so I could not just chase after him. So I stood at the door to try and keep him in my eyesight, called my wife, who went and got him home. Once we calmed down we called our agency caseworker to let them know what happened. We were then informed to call licensing at the state level. I then sat down and filled out a detailed report and notes of everything that happened. Within a day or so we got a call that licensing was coming in for an investigation. When they came in the case worker was very friendly. She opened her laptop since they record the whole interview. She then proceeded to ask me everything that happened. Most of the questioning was focused on ensuring we were doing our full due diligence to monitor all children and keep them safe at all times. There would be follow-up questions along the way. I never thought she was ever asking any "gotcha" questions, although I am sure some do. Next, the child gets interviewed by themselves. This may be the most nerve wracking moment. Then the caseworker checks a few things in your home to make sure you are following minimum standards and tells you that you will hear from them in a few days/weeks depending on the situation.

Obviously some situations call for longer investigations than others and some will involve a child being removed from the home temporarily or permanently. But the interview process will be part of all of them and know that no matter what happens you are not the first one to have that happen.

For the rest of the time you basically hold your breath. I wish I could say something nicer but that is literally what it can feel like. In most cases we have found that assuming you did everything you were supposed to, which you most likely ~~will~~ have, the worst case scenario is the child is moved to a different foster home. This can be heartbreaking, but I wanted you to know that typically the worst case scenarios that might creep into your mind just are not reality. Also, I want to help you realize that investigations are NOT fishing expeditions to try and get you. CPS is simply doing their due diligence to ensure that in the specific instance in question you were doing everything you could to care for the child.

Finally, what should you do? First off, always take detailed notes as a foster parent and fill out all required reports. This way you have detailed documentation of everything and not just a situation where you are under investigation. Next, if you are ever unsure of anything and what to do, contact your agency and/or caseworker. You also want to make sure you are fully honest about everything. The truth wins out in the long run.

The biggest key to coming through an investigation, and the most important thing you can do, your complete trust in God. He is in control. He is bigger than CPS or any situation that may come. So pray for God to be in control, pray for peace, pray for patience, and pray prayers of thankfulness for all God does to protect you and the kid. Trust that when the time comes you will have the words to say and the wisdom to take the appropriate actions.

I apologize but I cannot really think of a journal or daily challenge for today.
Maybe you could write down your biggest fears about investigations and lay them at the altar. But I mainly ask that you take time to pray for

foster parents facing investigations and the kids involved. Pray for strength, peace, calm, and wisdom. Pray for protection and for the truth to come out, whether the foster parent is wrongfully accused or truly in the wrong and needs to be moved or protected. And pray that all involved would have the strength to continue and carry on once the investigation is over. And just in case God reveals something you should journal about that I did not think of, space is provided.

_____

_____

_____

_____

_____

Daily Challenge: Keep Praying.

Day 19

Peacemakers

*Blessed are the peacemakers for they will be
called children of God.*
Matthew 5:9

My church recently did a series over the Sermon
on the Mount. One of the verses stuck out to
me. I think because it is counterintuitive to my
personality. "Blessed are the peacemakers for
they will be called children of God."
Peacemakers: that word kept bothering me. I
am not easily angered nor do I get upset often.
However I have a high sense of justice, and
when I see someone treated unfairly or getting
undeserved grief, it makes me ready for battle.
I want to let others know what they are doing is
wrong. I need them to immediately change and
be remorseful. Being a peacemaker sometimes
feels like a loss, like the battle wasn't really
won.

I know I do this with foster kids. I want them
to be treated fairly, as normal as possible. I
want others to see the child, not their problems.
As I thought about this verse I started thinking
about times when I went into situations not
being a peacemaker. I distinctly remember this

one time when dealing with the children's ministry at our church. We had a boy placed with us who had lots of struggles. The children's ministry at this time was not a safe place for him. It did not help him succeed. I wanted desperately for him to love being at church, for him to know God's unconditional love for him, and to see adults who loved Christ. I did not know what his future held but for the time he was in our house, I wanted him to learn these truths. Many things happened to him and there were things said about him while he was in the children's ministry that felt unfair to him. For example, he sometimes had accidents when he was anxious. A staff member was so upset with him that when she began to tell me, she could not remember his name and was talking loudly so anyone around could hear. She was not showing grace. I could tell she was annoyed and the child did too. He was so embarrassed. At one point we were told "other kids are so scared of him because he is different so I am not sure he can come back." Talk about angry tears!!! I was mad! I went straight to the boss's boss. I demanded better treatment, and apologies. I basically said if my kids are not welcome here then you guys are doing a bad job. Peacemaker, that was far from my attitude, far from my tone and my actions.

In return, I am not sure if this particular child ever felt safe at church[3].

As I look back, I am not sure I handled the situation correctly. Did action need to be taken? Yes. But was there a better way? Some of those workers are still at our church. I wish I would have been more of a peacemaker in this situation and calmly assessed the situation to come up with solutions. As foster parents, we can always feel like we are at war with those outside of the foster care world. A peacemaker does not run from conflict, is not passive, but is someone who seeks good over evil. Instead of handling conflict one-sided, we need to seek to build bridges. And isn't this what our children need? There is enough "war" in their life. We, as foster parents, can be the peacemaker for them in many areas. We can advocate and also be peacemakers.

Take some time to think if there is a situation you handled without being a peacemaker. Write down the ways you may have made it worse.

---

[3] I also would like to say that I do believe my church has taken huge steps and is more understanding and accommodating to kids from hard places. It's been a huge joy to see the change.

_____

_____

_____

_____

_____

Daily challenge: Pray and ask God how you can reconcile the above situation peacefully. And if you do not have anything to reconcile at this time, pray God will give you the attitude of a peacemaker when advocating for the children in your home.

Day 20

Complete Healing Comes From God

Surely he took up our pain and bore our suffering,
yet we considered him punished by God, stricken by
him, and afflicted. But he was pierced for our
transgressions, he was crushed for our iniquities;
the punishment that brought us peace was on him,
and by his wounds we are healed.
Isaiah 53:4-5

We live in a sinful world, and because of that sin our world is broken. Due to this brokenness, life is messy and sometimes downright messed up. At times this is because of decisions we make, other times it is decisions others make around us , and other times it is almost like we just get caught in the crossfire of all the brokenness. This was not God's intention. God designed us, and the world, to have perfect fellowship with Him. With sin that fellowship was broken, our world is broken, and we all deserve death and destruction. Here is the great part though! God did not want to leave things that way. He sent His Son to take on the pain, suffering, and death that we deserved so that we can find healing, restoration, and salvation. And, in case you did not know, complete healing can only come from God.

You cannot carry the burden for healing the children who come through your home on your own. It will take a team of caseworkers, friends, biological or adoptive parents, teachers, and counselors. Most importantly, it will also take God. We can chip away at the pain and brokenness and play a huge role in the lives of these children from hard places. At the end of the day, only God can completely heal them emotionally, physically, and spiritually.

Please find encouragement in these words. This is not all on you. With that knowledge, please be challenged to tap into that power. Please realize you are facing a real tangible battle as well as a spiritual one. So go to war for the children in your home.

I also want you to find encouragement in the fact that God does protect, heal and restore kids. There are so many ways we have seen this play out. We have had kids whose parents blamed them for their problems leading to intense neglect. These kids were never physically touched or enrolled in school or activities. By the time they left our homes, they were happy and testing for the gifted/talented program at their new school. We have had kids who were so filled with anger, frustration, and confusion they could not survive a day at school. Eventually they had to be removed from our home. But they went on to learn to cope and find a forever family. We have had kids who faced unspeakable abuse and somehow God protected the from fully grasping what was happening so that they could still live a happy childhood and find healing. Maybe most of all, with all of the placements we have had, I have seen a sense of resiliency that could only have come from God. There is no other explanation that makes sense.

Think about it. Not only are you pulled from your parents but then you are having to talk to all sorts of strangers and bounce from home to home. You have to process what is happening in your life. Yet somehow they continue to thrive. I do not know if I could do that as an adult, let alone as a kid.

God is big. God wants to bring healing. God is the only one who can bring full healing. God will bring full healing. Today write down ways God has brought healing in your life and/or the lives of the children in your home and praise Him for that.

_____

_____

_____

_____

_____

Daily Challenge: In at least 5 conversations today give credit to God for something good in your life or the lives of the kids in your home.

Day 21

Guest Contributor
Amy Curtis, Director Of Counseling For Buckner
International

Amy, as well as serving the families of Buckner, is a doctoral candidate in family therapy. Amy's expertise in her field has guided us in a better understanding of how to love and nurture our children.

In Numbers 11, Moses takes his burdens, his exhaustion and his needs to the Lord. He just cannot do it anymore. He states he would rather die than carry the burdens of the people on his shoulders any longer. In his conversation with God, he sounds angry, almost sarcastic ("Did I conceive all these people?").

What you learn from Moses, Stephanie and Buck is the importance of authenticity. Being real with God. As a therapist for Buckner, I can try desperately to help those who are struggling, to foster healing for those who have been harmed, and to encourage those who are exhausted and depleted. But if they are not able to see their needs clearly or willing to accept help the therapeutic relationship is strained or non-existent. Our relationship with God requires authenticity. God knew Moses needed help but He also waited for Moses to ask for help. And God did not hesitate to meet Moses's need once he asked.

In addition, in this passage between Moses and God, God did not shame Moses for asking for help, or for his anger. He did not say "What is the matter with you, Moses? I asked you to do one thing and you aren't doing it." Nor did Moses go back to God and say "No worries, God. I've got it." Instead, the Lord told Moses to gather together those he trusted and The Lord anointed them to serve alongside Moses. This is the community that Stephanie and Buck have been describing. You will need this community. Moses already knew who to gather together. He knew the leaders. He knew who he and others could trust. I highly recommend you pull together your most trusted leaders and those who will serve beside you. But, remember, your willingness to ask for help, and to be real about your strengths, your weaknesses and your needs, can make or break your ability to serve those God has entrusted to your care.

Amy Curtis
Director Of Counseling For Buckner international

Day 22

Perseverance

Let us not lose heart in doing good, for in due time we will reap a harvest if we do not grow weary.
Galatians 6:9

Yet those who wait for the LORD Will gain new strength; They will mount up with wings like eagles, They will run and not get tired, They will walk and not become weary.
Isaiah 40:3

Today, I want to talk about feeling spiritually tired. As I have said before, I really was not a weeper until I became a foster parent. Sure I have cried, but truly weeping was something I gained from being a parent. When you hear the stories we hear, and you do the work we do, it's hard to not become spiritually tired. This work is hard. Each time a child leaves your home, the reality of the situation is that another will come. The work sometimes feels like it will never be done. In truth, until Jesus returns, the work is never done. As long as sin is still in our world, the work is never done.

The first time we left a child at the psychiatric hospital at 1 a.m., I wept. I wept the whole way home, the whole night and then on my way back to visit him the next day. I found the strength not to cry while I visited him. A worker said, "Oh, you came to visit him? Foster kids usually don't have visitors." Then I cried some more.

This work is so hard, and at times, my spirit gets tired and weary. I was weary many times in our journey. And as my husband and I pray about reopening our home soon, my biggest concern is about being weary, and feeling hopeless. These two verses above keep coming to mind. It's almost like God is giving me a pep talk at halftime of a big game. Do not lose heart in doing good! Good will happen. I desperately need to hear this at times. I need to be reminded God is in the business of doing good! Just remembering He is good takes the pressure off of me and puts it on Him.

I also love how Isaiah 40:3 talks about waiting on the Lord. Part of what makes foster care hard is all the waiting...waiting for decisions to be made, waiting for answers, waiting for healing, waiting for the doctor, waiting for caseworkers, waiting for counselors, and the list goes on. But have you seen an eagle fly? They fly as if they own the sky and rule it. As a follower of Christ we know who rules the world, Jesus! He is our strength and with Him, only with Him, can we do this work. Make sure you take time to fill your spirit with His promises and truths, spending time in prayer conversing with him, taking time to be still and know that He is God (Psalms 46:10).

Take time today to write down areas where your spirit may feel weary. It may be trying to handle a kid's behavior, waiting on the court for a decision, or just wrestling with the big hurt the child(ren) in your home have gone though.

_____

_____

_____

_____

_____

Daily challenge: Pray that God will renew your spirit in these areas and ask him to show you His goodness.

Day 23

Rest

"Come to me, all you who are weary and burdened, and I will give you rest. Take my yoke upon you and learn from me, for I am gentle and humble in heart, and you will find rest for your souls. For my yoke is easy and my burden is light."
Matthew 11:28-30

If God took a day off, shouldn't we? If God commanded us to rest, why don't we? He even promised us that if we came to Him, He would give us rest. How can this be? How can choosing the way of doing all the work God is calling us too give us rest? This seems especially counterintuitive as foster parents. With all the extra challenges that get thrown into our days and the trials the kids in our homes are often facing, the idea that the way we are choosing is easier than the life of those around us seems idiotic. It is true because when we trust in God and do things His way, we are not doing things alone. So we can persevere through the trials we are facing. Realizing this, we can find rest in the midst of the war.

Likewise, we must find time for rest in between the wars. This may look like tagging out when a spouse comes home from work and walking away for a little bit. It may mean you reach out to a friend or neighbor to watch your kids so you can take a breather. You may need to take advantage of respite every once in awhile. And you definitely might need to take a break between placements. If you do not find time for rest, you will burn out. Rest is a Biblical principle, so we know the need for it is a reality. But, I also know it from experience.

I cannot remember the last time I was good at resting. When it comes to work or online business, I am always thinking of the next thing to do. I like to run and train for endurance races, and my least favorite day is the rest day I have to take once a week. Worst of all, in our journey of Foster Care And Adoption, I never took time to rest. If we had a placement go home, I went back to work the next day. When we had a failed adoption and got kicked out of court on a Friday, I went back to work on a Monday. When there was a kid throwing a massive fit at home, I let everyone else leave and I stayed back with them. Because of this, I not only got compassion fatigue, I got compassion burnout.

I learned about these conditions through a training we were required to do. Basically your tank has only so much ability to care for others and if you keep emptying it without taking time to refill it you either get fatigued and must sit out from caring for a while, or you get burned out and have to sit out for a long while. For me I had gone so long without resting, processing, and recovering that when our last placement left, an extremely difficult one I might add, I was finished. And I mean I was completely done caring. I remember telling my wife, "I will love you and I will love our kids but I am done loving anyone else." That included our small group at church and our immediate family. Please know this did not mean I hated them, but it meant I had nothing left in the tank to muster up in order to serve them or listen to their hurts and struggles. At the time I did not know I had compassion burnout. I just knew I was empty. It took me a long time to come back and it is still a struggle some time. It felt like coming back from the flu. Even after the cause of the sickness is gone, it still takes a while to replenish your body. Then after you've refueled, you're not at full strength for a long time, and can easily relapse if you are not careful.

I do not want this for any of you. Please do not try to be a hero. Please do not think you are being more spiritual by not taking a break. You are hero enough just by committing to do what God has called you to do. You must find times for rest both in the war and outside of it. This must be a spiritual discipline that you do not sacrifice.

Today in your journal space build out a "non-negotiable" rest plan. I use quotes because real life can change any plans, but I want you to work out how you want to handle tagging out in crisis moments, how long of a break you think you should take between placements, list what foster parents you can reach out to for advice, how often you want to have a night out or weekend away, and any other ways or times that you think you might need rest. This is not about taking the easy road or avoiding your responsibilities. This is about keeping yourself and your relationships healthy so you can be in the journey for the long haul.

_____

_____

_____

_____

_____

Daily Challenge: Discuss this list with your spouse, or if you are single with your most trusted, reliable friend or family member in your support system. Through those discussions refine your list and save it or even frame it. Then put it somewhere that you will see it regularly as a reminder of not only your need to rest but also how you plan to do it.

Day 24

Unconditional Love

*"Who shall separate us from the love of Christ?
Shall trouble or hardship or persecution or
famine or nakedness or danger or sword? As it
is written: "For your sake we face death all day
long; we are considered as sheep to be
slaughtered." No, in all these things we are
more than conquerors through him who loved
us. For I am convinced that neither death nor
life, neither angels nor demons, neither the
present nor the future, nor any powers, neither
height nor depth, nor anything else in all
creation, will be able to separate us from the
love of God that is in Christ Jesus our Lord."*
Romans 8:35-39

I remember sitting outside watching a particular
6 year old calm down from a tantrum. This
child had big emotions for such a little kid. On
this particular night, he was trying to climb our
one tree in the backyard so he could hop the
fence and runaway. Anything was better than
living with us. I sat on our porch watching him
to make sure he didn't harm himself and using
our de-escalation techniques which had been
taught in our trainings. Nothing seemed to be
working. I kept thinking: "How did he get to

this type of anger?" "How do I teach a 6 year old to trust a stranger?" "How do I show him appropriate love?" "If he does make it over that fence, what am I allowed to do to make sure he comes back safely?"

As I am running through all of these scenarios, praying he is too weak to pull himself over the fence, I hear a calm voice say, "Mom, what happens if I do run away?" Inside I really wanted to say, "Well, you will be in huge trouble!" Somehow, instead, I answered, "I will be sad and scared so I will call the police to help find you and they will bring you back here." Then he said, "Ok, but what if I run away again after they bring me back?" And I again answer, "I will be scared and sad so I will call the police to have them help again and they will bring you back here." A third time he asks, "So if I run away after that will you call again and let me come back?" I remember thinking, "Yes, I have said this twice already! Just get down! But I said, "Of course, I will always ask the police to bring you back here. This is your home right now." He looks at me and says, "Ok, well, then I better just get down and stay here."

He thanks me and goes on about the rest of his night as if nothing happened.   When I think about how many times a child from a hard place has to be reminded of their value, I sometimes feel overwhelmed or tired, as if they should just get it by now. However, I am then reminded of how many times we fail God, our Creator, our Savior. Apart from denying Him, His Word says nothing can separate us from His love. We cannot do anything to earn His love more or do anything to lose His love.

The children who are sharing our home with us most likely have never had someone show them unconditional love. A love not attached to performance. A love that cannot be lost. Take some time to think and/or write down some of the ways God showed you His unconditional love.

_____

_____

_____

_____

_____

Daily Challenge: When the children in your home make a poor choice, get on your nerves today, or show their big emotions, think of how our Father's love is unconditional and how you too do not deserve His love. Take a breath or two before you react and show unconditional love to them.

Day 25

Going the extra Mile

Whoever forces you to go one mile, go with him two.
Matthew 5:41

I am not sure where I first learned about the Roman law that allowed Roman soldiers to ask a civilian to carry their bags for a mile.   In Matthew, we read about this law and then Jesus asks us to not only go the one mile required but to go ahead and do another mile. To go above and beyond to show kindness. What does this mean in foster care? How can we go the extra mile when we already are required to do so much?

For us, in one case, this meant we had the opportunity to really love on the birth mom. I do not even remember how our relationship with mom began. She spoke little English and I speak even less Spanish. I began to give her written updates on her children and how they were growing and doing in our home. When the children went home, we were sad but happy for her. Mom would let the kids call us, and we got to stay in contact with them. On one of the visits mom was telling me she was having a hard time grocery shopping and knowing how to feed her children. I had been praying since the kids left that God would protect them and keep them safe. I remember thinking, "Well this is not protecting them." But as God often does, He urged me to see things differently, and instead I offered to take mom shopping and show her just how to shop and provide meals on a budget. It was a blessing to see a mom wanting to learn and wanting to take care of her children. My attitude towards mom became one of wanting her to succeed; instead of afraid she was going to fail.

In previous days we have talked about God's forgiveness for all, His complete healing and now this idea of going the extra mile. I truly believe when we go the extra mile for others, our attitude towards them changes. If you go the extra mile you are setting up for success, and isn't this what we want for others (or should want)?

Take some to time to identify the area God is wanting you to go the extra mile in. It may be doing extra counseling sessions that are not required, or learning about your child's heritage so you can teach them about it, or having some contact with the birth family (when appropriate). Today, write out ways you can go the extra mile for your children.

_____

_____

_____

_____

_____

Daily Challenge: Pray for willingness and that
you will take advantage of the opportunities to
go the extra mile. Then, do it!

Day 26

Boundaries

You are the body of Christ. Each one of you is a part of it.
1 Corinthians 12:17

Take some time to read the entire chapter of 1 Corinthians 12. As you read the chapter, remember that we are all in this together. When you mourn, we mourn, and when you rejoice, we rejoice. If you ever need support, information or whatever, we and other foster and adoptive parents are happy to provide what you need. That is just part of being in the foster care/adoptive community. This community extends to churches, caseworkers, counselors, teachers, and all sorts of other people in your life, including the children in your home.

More importantly, for today at least, I want you to realize that you play an important role in that community. A specific role. You do not, and should not, have to do everything. You have specific skills and a specific job to do and that job will be done in specific timing. Yes, you will hear about a laundry list of opportunities and countless stories of hurt. But you cannot do everything, you cannot be everywhere, you cannot fix every problem, nor should you.

Let that free you for a moment. You have a job to do, and you need to do it well. You do not have to do every job or someone else's job. You may want to put that on a mirror or somewhere you look every day. Because at times in the foster care and adoptive journey you will need to be reminded of that. This does not mean life will be easy but remembering this truth will help you to avoid veering off from God's call for you, hurting those close to you or the kids in your home, and experiencing burnout.

I (Buck) wish that someone had taught me this lesson early on because with our first placement, I definitely could have used it. Our first placement was a two week old baby girl and a 3 year old little boy. Very quickly it was like we bonded as family, especially me and the little girl. This is partially because within 24 hours of the placement Stephanie got a stomach bug and I was in charge. After 8 months in our home they went home. This was a good thing but it was hard to let go.

Since we had a relationship with mom we felt the right thing to do was to continue to help. We babysat so mom could go to work, gave her a baby crib, toys, and other things. This may have been the right thing to do if we had set some boundaries. Anytime mom called, it did not matter what story she told us, I came running. Even when we had a placement of two other kids, one of them with some serious struggles, I would leave and go pick up all six of her kids. Probably deep down because I needed to check on "my little girl". There was even one night we had literally just left the little boy who was placed with us at a psychiatric hospital and the mom from our first placement gave us a call. Well guess what? I grabbed a car seat, left my wife to go pick up the boy's little sister at the babysitter, and went to pick up the kids. Now it was a misunderstanding where she just wanted to talk to us about something else, but nonetheless I had gone running. This added emotional stress to those around me, especially the kids. This lack of boundaries was a big part of contributing to my eventual burnout. It meant that the two kids in my home who desperately needed healing probably did not get all the full attention they needed. It also meant that when our original placement came back to our home and mom asked us to adopt them, but she later changed her mind, I probably was not seeing clearly about what was God's will. It meant that getting over the emotional pain of those two children going home again took so much longer.

It is so hard to put on paper how much not having boundaries cost us. I hope you can realize that while going the extra mile is part of being a foster parent, you also need to have boundaries and realize that you have specific jobs to do in specific time frames. Because without this, you will become no good to anyone while you are trying to be good to everyone.

Today journal some of your strengths and weaknesses in setting boundaries.

_____

_____

_____

_____

_____

Daily Challenge: Write a letter to yourself as a challenge and reminder when you need it about how you will find balance between going the extra mile and boundaries and why it is important.

Day 27

Joy!

Consider it all joy, my brethren, when you encounter various trials, knowing that the testing of your faith produces endurance. And let endurance have its perfect result, so that you may be perfect and complete, lacking in nothing.
James 1:2-4

Let me be honest. Writing this devotional has been a bittersweet journey for me. I have had to relive some hard stories, remind myself of the children that have come and gone from our home, and know that with most of them I do not know where they are and how they are doing. My emotions have been all over the place. Maybe like me, you have thought, "Why did my family decide to do this, to invite chaos, uncertainty, and pain into our lives?"

But, my friends, I tell you in all the questioning, the pain, the emotions, the paperwork, the uncertainty brings the above verse to life for me. I don't think I ever understood how someone can experience joy during trials and testing of faith until we chose to open our home to do foster care. This journey has been the reason for some big hurt, but also big joy. As I relived the stories of our kids and it brought some tears of pain, it would be a disservice to God if I did not talk about the joy in the pain that we experienced.

Just a few of our joys include: two of our forever children, friends we would have never had otherwise, children healing, seeing children learn to ride a bike, swim, learning to talk, walk, and even smile again! These things are pure joy. The joy that comes during pain, the reasons why we do what we do. I have had many people ask would you do this again, is the pain worth it? YES! A thousand times, yes.

Take time to write down the joy foster care has brought to your family and the joy you are currently experiencing in your journey.

_____

_____

_____

_____

_____

Daily challenge: There is no better way to end today than by asking God to continually show you the JOY in the trials and for the energy to persevere. I know foster care is a world many understand, but what an opportunity you have to see God work in a world that feels very dark at times, a world where evil happens to even the littlest of children. What a privilege it is for Him to use us. I thank God, and pray you will too, for allowing foster care to be a part of our journey, part of our life and our story.

Day 28

Guest Contributor
Madeline Reedy, Senior Director, TRAC

Madeline works diligently to serve youth who have aged out of care. She has grown and shaped her program to be the best in Texas (in our opinion). Madeline is also a personal friend of ours and has shown compassion, understanding and encouragement as we foster children.

Over the last sixteen years, I've met thousands of youth in the child welfare system. Each one carries their own story, woven with trauma, personality, and grit. A single account would fail to adequately describe them all. However, I want to provide some insight into my unique vantage point. Most of my experience is with young adults ages 16 to 24 who never found permanency, whose adoptions failed, or who chose to never be adopted. I oversee City Square's Transition Resource Action Center (TRAC), whose mission is to help those who exit systems of care find self-sufficiency. 99% of the youth we help age out of the foster care system. When I first tell people about TRAC, they are surprised. Most people, and maybe you too, think of sweet babies in foster care who find their forever home. For a grand majority, that is true. But every year, thousands exit the child welfare system at age 18 without a parent to guide them. Statistics are bleak for this group of young adults. They are disproportionately at risk for homelessness, poverty, unemployment, trafficking, unwed parenthood, and criminal engagement. When they arrive at TRAC's door, 50% have experienced homelessness; 46% are without a GED or Diploma; 70% are unemployed; and 52% have no source of income.

I tell you this not to discourage you, but to help you understand how vital your role is in the child welfare system. Sometimes I'm asked by various groups what they can do to help TRAC. Each time, I disappoint our development department because I usually fail to mention the ways they can get involved in our program. Overwhelmingly, I respond with the most needed thing for this community at large – more investment by individuals into the work. Exactly what you are doing! The best way to create better outcomes for youth as they age out is for there to be more foster/adoptive parents and CASA advocates. When we can build capacity to where every young person in care is in a loving, trained foster home and each one has an unpaid volunteer speaking for them in court, those youth are more likely to stay in one home, be connected to a community, and find a caring adult. With those elements in their pocket, their ability to find their way vastly improves.

Right now, most youth who age out didn't enter foster care until they were between the ages of 11 -15, which means a tragedy occurred for the system to get involved. Once in care, they have on average 8 placements, which means they move every 6 months, and have around 5 caseworkers, meaning a new one every year. Such disruption after a traumatic event builds a sense of insecurity, unrest, and inability to focus on school and other positive experiences. We need you, committed foster parents desperately.

I thank you for choosing this work. I know it is hard, and some days impossible. I hope this study encourages you and helps you find ways to keep the faith. You are doing God's own work. You are bringing hope to those who are most in need. We're all in this together. May Isaiah 41 encourage you as your involvement encourages me.

For the youth,
Madeline Reedy
Senior Director, TRAC
www.citysquare.org/trac

Made in the USA
Middletown, DE
04 May 2018